You Have Heard It Said, Every Book Tells a Story

Teresa Holt

Order this book online at www.trafford.com
or email orders@trafford.com

Most Trafford titles are also available at major online book retailers.

Printed in the United States of America.

ISBN: 978-1-4669-5922-4 (sc)
ISBN: 978-1-4669-5923-1 (e)

Trafford rev. 10/01/2012

 www.trafford.com

North America & international
toll-free: 1 888 232 4444 (USA & Canada)
phone: 250 383 6864 ♦ fax: 812 355 4082

I hope you all will be blessed and find this book to be encouraging.

I also hope you will find inspiration in this very special year 2012

Your light to shine forth in the darkness as a beacon to all nations.

By the blood of the lamb and by the word of our testimonies we are over comers able to minister to others salvation and forgiveness which works through us.

The blanket of stars in the sky above shows the magnificants of you. For we are a mere dot on the page compared to the magnitude of you.

The water is a well of water springing up into everlasting life, for it is written and its true let the light live in you forever be with your God.

Contents

Scripture I heard a voice from heaven
Poem for my youngest sister

Nicolia is my sister . . . she is younger than me.
She has two sisters and a brother
In their fifties.

Now its my sisters turn . . . she has reached the big 5.0
And I hope and pray she has many more to go.
It doesn't matter what she says
Or even what she does because even when we
Seem far apart
Nicolia is always in my heart.

I don't think she quite understands
The feelings that I have got
So I would like to tell you all right now
I love that girl a lot.

Chapter 1

***

Introducing myself

I have two younger sisters and one older brother, our parents always went to church, the church of England where we attended the Sunday school. I remember on one of the Sundays the teacher handed us all a piece of paper with a few lines of scripture written on each one.

We had to learn the lines before the following Sunday, mine was herein, herein is love not that we loved God but that God loves us, he sent his son into the world for the transgressions of our sins. I felt quite shy and it took a lot of courage for me to stand in front of the congregation but I managed it.

I was still quite young when my parents bought a new house for us all to live in, on the moving in day we were all told when we arrive we must all carry something in with us but as we pulled up in the car I wanted to go to the toilet so I made a dash for it, I proceeded to run up the stairs when everything seemed to go into slow motion, I looked up to the top of the stairs, a man was standing there wearing a dark suit and a hat on his head, I thought, he must be helping my mum and dad move in, I looked back towards the front door and then back at the man, who at this time was only a few steps away from me,I thought that's strange I didn't hear him coming down the stairs, I moved closer to the wall to give him room to pass me but as he passed I still didn't feel a thing. The front door had been closed by this time and as the man stood in front of the door he looked up at me smiled took of his hat bowed his head put the hat back on patted it and walked straight through the door, I started screaming, my dad came out of the front room and asked, what is wrong, I explained what had happened, later my mum said its alright he just came to see that we had moved in alright, he's gone now.

As I reached my teens a lot of people that I knew was aloud out until quite late, I was given a time to be in always earlier than my friends, this led me to be always late in, my parents would ground me for a while let me out and the same thing would happen all over again.

One night they were having live music playing in a pub we all decided to go. I was bought a lot of drinks and not being a drinker it went straight to my head and worse when I went outside in the fresh air. As I went outside with a couple of friends there seemed to be a lot of boys hanging around, I was dragged over the road into the field on the other side, I was thrown down on the ground and raped.

I was crying out help me make it stop, make them go away, it seemed to carry on for some time, I started pleading inside father I am sorry help me, with that I must have past out as the next thing I knew I could just about make out the shadows of people walking away, I thought thank God, then I thought don't make a sound just in-case they come back, when I knew it was quiet and I couldn't see anything moving I tried to stand up and make my way to the road and as I stood up a man was standing there, I thought oh no here we go again but I noticed the time had gone just as it did before in slow motion, the man said let me help you as he stretched out his hand, I shouted at him to go away again the voice said let me help you, I said leave me alone, go away, with that he was gone, I looked across the field, all around me to see if I could see anyone walking away but no, there wasn't anyone. For years after this although it was terrifying and a horrible experience I felt more upset at the fact I told someone to go away who wanted to help me. Forgiveness kept coming up as I read the bible, forgive others as I forgive you, I wasn't in the mood to forgive but after some time I thought there is no point holding on to this. I forgave and then you can move on and truly you can say father forgive them, and forgive me also.

Chapter 2

I started going to a club for children where I met a boy, he bought me a coke and asked me if he could walk me home I said no. We would speak on several occasions as we would bump into each other in town I told him my family and me are moving to Australia as he kept asking me to go out with him.

After the last time I saw him, we moved to Australia, I didn't see him again until a few years later, I worked in a factory making trousers at my first job in Australia, I had to keep up with the girls on the machines by cutting the material between each trouser and turning them inside out, I got blisters on my hands and I knew I was going slow so the manager asked me to leave which I was thankful for, my next job was in a hotel I loved working there, I was taught a lot from everyone who worked with me at this time, we had a swimming pool that we would always be in swimming and messing around.

After a few years in Australia my parents decided to come back to England although it's a fantastic place we was all pleased to be coming back. it wasn't long before I caught up with some of my friends and the boy who kept asking me out, well we did go out together and we did get married. We lived with his parents as the place we was going to move into fell through. While I was writing this book my sons found out that their dad had lost his leg and he had terminal cancer, they were desperate to see him, one day when my husband and myself were shopping we bumped into him, he spoke to my sons on the phone and to our grandson, they all was quite emotional we arranged to pick him up so that he could stay with our eldest son for the following weekend

He told them that he loved them very much and was sorry for everything, which did them all good. We spoke about Jesus Christ and the forgiveness that we are shown from our Lord, he wouldn't let us pray for him openly but we can pray for him in secret . . .

Scripture

Our hope is steadfast, yes we had the
Sentence of death in ourselves
That we should not trust in ourselves but
In God who raises the dead
Faith and hope in Jesus Christ
The son of the living God
Who when we are faithless
He remains faithful

God commanded light to shine
Out of darkness
Who has shone in our hearts
To give the light of the knowledge
Of the glory of God in the face of
Jesus Christ.

But we have this treasure in earthen
Vessels that the excellence of the power
May be of God and not of us.

You know the grace of our Lord
Jesus Christ that though he was rich
Yet for our sakes he became poor
That you through his poverty might
Become rich.

Introducing myself

Many years went past when I met a man and although we both didn't want to get together, we did, we got married, he is the most wonderful man you could meet, I love him very much.

We had always spoke about Jesus Christ, prayed about different things we didn't actually go to church.

We started to read the bible with Jehovahs witnesses they would come to our house once a week we really enjoyed our time with them, we had some very good discussions.

It was about this time that I was seeking after the truth, I would pray and ask what is the right way. what is the truth. Every time I opened the bible it would be at the verse, I am the way I am the truth I am the life no one goes to the father only through me. It was around this time I heard the song behold the man upon the cross my sin upon his shoulders ashamed I hear my mocking voice call out among the scoffers it was my sin that held him there until it was accomplished his dying breath has bought me life. I had heard this song, I don't know how many times over the years, I would have a cry and that would be that but this time I fell on my knees and asked for forgiveness for the first time I could see how pure, free from sin this Jesus Christ was and that he came for a wretch like me. I cried and cried it was if the vail had been lifted, and at this time Jesus Christ became my lord my saviour my God.

My dad was driving around looking for somewhere to go when he heard singing he thought it sounded so good he will follow the singing and go inside.

He did and when my dad saw us he said come along you will enjoy it, at this time I was waiting to go into hospital to have a piece of bowel removed. we went along to the outreach and anyone was welcome to go to the front for prayer, my dad kept saying you go, I said no then my dad just pulled me into the isle. I thought there is no way I am going to fall onto the ground as I have seen so many people do. The Pastor prayed for me and as I started to walk away my legs went weak, I was on the floor. When I got home, I opened the bible to faith without works are dead and without faith it is impossible to please God.

I thought instead of putting my trust into the Lord healing me and just receiving the prayer I was mocking in a way by thinking I'm not going to be pushed. I'm not going on the floor how stupid could I get.

A few weeks later I went into hospital for my operation. when I came back from the theatre I had an epidural in my back, I was in agony from just under my chest to my groin, I had no feelings in my both my legs at all. I asked the nurse if I could have the epidural removed, I said I am in a lot of pain, but I have no feelings in my legs. the nurse went away in a very short time she returned, she said she had asked the surgeon and he wanted me to keep it in for a while longer as this was my only form of pain killer, my husband came to visit me and started to rub my legs this brought the feelings back into them and the epidural was taken out, I couldn't sleep or get comfortable for days the pain was unbearable, I cried out in my spirit Lord please take this pain away but more or less at the same time I thought you suffered for me and I am asking you to take the pain from me. Then I said if I could just go to sleep that would be something, with that I must have fallen asleep, I didn't wake until the following morning, I thought I will go outside to get some fresh air and have a cigarette.

On one of the times that I was on my way out one of the nurses called me, I thought oops she is going to tell me off.

But she said there is a gentleman in the side room there pointing at the room. she said he wants you to go and see him, I don't know why I just didn't go because that's what I normally would have done but instead I said tell him to come out side for some fresh air, the nurse said he has lost both of his legs I said that's alright tell him to come outside, I carried on and went outside, not long afterwards a man in a wheelchair came up to me he said is that right you told me to come outside to see you I said yes, he said you will not know this they have been trying to get me out of my bed for ages but I wouldn't move I was so depressed until I kept seeing your smiling face every time you past my room. I said I need to talk to that girl as you past my room and you making me come out here to talk to you is what I needed. Thank you.

We spoke about God and I hope he went on to be in good health.

Chapter 3

Chapter 3

Scripture

Now thanks be to God who always leads us in triumph

In Christ and through us diffuses the fragrance of his knowledge in every place

For we are to God the fragrance of Christ among those who are being saved
and to those who are perishing

To one we are aroma of death leading to death

And to the other the aroma of life leading to life

And who is sufficient for these things for we are not as so many pending the
word of God

But as of sincerity but as from God we speak in the sight of God in Christ

Treasure in earthen vessels knowing that, he raised up the Lord Jesus will also
raise us up with Jesus and will present us with you.

That grace having spread through many may cause

Thanks-giving to abound to the glory of God.

Therefore we do not lose heart even though our outward man is perishing, yet
the inward man is being renewed day by day

For our light affliction, which is for a moment, is working for us a far more
exceeding and eternal weight of glory

While we do not look at the things which are seen but at the things which are
not seen, for the things which are seen are temporary but the things which
are not seen are eternal.

For we know that if our earthly house a building from God a house not made
with hands, eternal in the heavens, earnestly desiring to be clothed with our
habitation which is from heaven, he has prepared us for this very thing.

Who also has given us a guarantee, pleasing to him,

The Holy Spirit.

Chapter 4

Testimony

Both my husband and myself was baptised at the Emmanuel church shortly afterwards the leaders of this church moved to Wales before they moved they introduced us to four leaders who were going to take over, the name was changing to marvellous light. we always had mid-week meetings to pray for the queen, family friends government and each other on one of the meetings one of our elderly ladies said that she had been suffering from gout and although she was on medication from her doctors the pain wasn't going away.

Our leader said Terry and Teresa will pray for anyone who needs prayer to night, as my husband and I stood up we could feel the presence of the holy spirit and knew this lady was going to feel the love of God in a way that she hadn't felt before.

Before we even put our hands upon her, she fell back into the arm chair and cried she said nobody knows this but I have been a Christian for years but I have never felt the power of God until now, the pain had left her, we just kept thanking the Lord we were so happy for her.

On that Sunday our leader said again if anyone wants prayer this morning Terry and Teresa will pray for you.

There were quite a few people in the queue one was a little Boy he was just about to go into hospital for a hernia operation, as my husband and myself put our hands upon him you could feel the hernia go back into place. the next week the boys mother said she didn't know if she should still take her son to the hospital or not but on the day of the operation the doctors said they would do another x-ray first. She said they came to speak to her and said there is nothing wrong with your baby, they cannot find anything.

On the same Sunday another lady came forward, we knew she wanted to feel the same as the lady on the Wednesday night, we didn't know at the time that they were sisters she said she had never felt like that in all the years that she had been a Christian, and when her sister told her how she felt on the Wednesday night she said she had to come and see for her self.

We found out later that these two sisters are prayer warriors, they both are truly wonderful ladies a joy to be around such a delight.

Chapter 5

Scripture

He takes away the first that he may establish the second
Jesus Christ came as a high priest of good things to come
with the greater and more perfect tabernacle.
Not made with hands nor of this creation
But with his own blood
He entered the most high place
Once for all, from dead works to serve the living
God, second time apart from sin for salvation.
The heavens declare his righteousness
And his truth endureth to all.

Introducing myself

We sometimes had a get together in the evening, for everyone to just have fellowship together, sing songs, poems, and just have a good time together. We also would have something to eat so we all agreed to have a buffet. I said I would do the food, on the morning I felt fine but as the hours past I felt as if I had flu coming or a cold, I took some lemsip and hoped this would pass.

I carried on making the food but I felt worse, I thought, I have to get the food finished and take it to the place where we are all meeting, as I didn't want to let anyone down. I just managed to finish getting everything together as my husband came in from work, he said you look awful, but we both decided to take the food and then come straight home.

When we arrived quite a few people were already there they didn't want us to go home and said let us pray for you, they did, but said I would be better off at home, at this time I could hardly keep my eyes open. As we were driving home I felt worse, when we finally arrived home I went straight to bed with a hot water bottle and then I had a dream.

I dreamed that I was climbing thousands of stars and every time I thought I can not go any further a voice would sound, come here, I would start to climb again the very moment I wanted to stop the voice would say again, come here, this went on it seemed for hours until the voice said, who do you seek after, I said, my father I want to thank him for giving me his son Jesus Christ.

With that split second I was standing at the side of a massive water fall, I was trying to make out what this could be as I noticed Jewels, Emeralds, Crystals when a voice came from the centre and said, come here, do you doubt, which I was so I just let myself fall into the water.

I felt myself falling but then what I thought was a water fall was a wing, I could here the sound like a loud woo-sh ing sound that covered me.

When I woke up my husband said, he had been really worried about me, I said I feel alright now, he said, I was just about to phone the doctors to see if someone could come out to see you. My husband carried on to say do you know how long you have been like this, I said no, he said three days,

I told my husband about the dream we couldn't make out what it meant.

After a few days I wrote the words down to drink to me only from my cup and I will drink with thee, for I am with you forever more and for eternity, I knew this to be a song.

But I still didn't know why or if anything had to come from this, I did a lot of praying and I just cannot explain the joy I felt.

Then I started writing the words down to my first poem at the time I didn't know if it would be a song or a poem, then the words to my second song.

Chapter 6

Poem

We meet with the heavenly hosts to sing praises
To our king
Yeshua we worship you for you are everything

Jesus we weep at your feet just like Mary
Your mother did
My soul cries out to you my lord
My redeemer lives

We shout glory be to the lamb on high
He has washed us with his blood
Jesus we bow before you and thank you
For your love

Have faith my little children to move in what
I give power comes from above
Because I am who I say I am
And that I live yes I am who I say I am
And that I live.

Song—Lord your spirit leads me.

Father you was there from the start
As a child I spoke to you
I did not comprehend from the start how much
I needed you no not until I grew

Lord your spirit leads me into your perfect love
Father I want to thank you in the truth that's from above

Lord you said you would never depart
So I put my trust in you
You're my shepherd and my Messiah
Most of all my saviour to my lord and saviour to

Lord your spirit leads me into your perfect love
Father I want to thank you in the truth that's from above

Carry me and my weary heart lift me up when
I am down you're the light when the world
Is so dark Jesus I see your crowns Jesus you
Wear the crowns

Lord your spirit leads me into your perfect love
Father I want to thank you in the truth that's from above

Now I would not have turned to you except you first
Loved me
My sin and my flesh have died
As you have set me free Jesus you set me free

Lord your spirit leads me into your perfect love
Father I want to thank you in the truth that's from above.

I didn't know what I had to do with these words but I knew it was all going to be revealed in time, when one Sunday the leader at our church said people will start to write down words to songs, they may not be musical or in be involved with anything to do with music but suddenly they will start to write words down, well my husband said Teresa has already written two songs our leader said bring them in so I worship leader can put music to them.

Chapter 7

Everyone more or less at this time was handing in
    songs that they had written it was fantastic.
We had two worship leaders and as soon as I gave
Them Lord your spirit leads me and I hear the sound,
They played a tune by strumming their guitars and
    made a c.d. with these and others on.
The third song that I wrote was
we sing hallelujah to you Lord
that was filmed one night when we did an outreach

Song—we sing hallelujah to you Lord

We sing hallelujah to you lord
as we lift our hands to you
We sing hallelujah way out loud
as we praise your mighty name
for you are the two edged sword
coming in all your glory soon
We sing hallelujah to you

its Jesus name above all names
yes its Jesus name above all names
we will stand fast and we will proclaim
that its Jesus name above all names

we give praise and thanks to you lord
you have given us everlasting life
with your blood you washed us white as snow
when you died on the cross that day
you did all of this for us
so that we may enter in
yes enter into your holy place

its Jesus name above all names
yes its Jesus name above all names
we will stand fast and we will proclaim
that its Jesus name above all names

I am the lord your God I reach out my hands to you
I will cover you under my wing
If your weary then come on in.

Song 4 that I wrote
I hear the sound

I hear the sound of my heart beat
When I think of you and I am at your feet
For my heart aches standing at the cross
Sharing with you suffering with you
Enduring what you went through

But the joy overwhelms me as your
Holy Spirit tells me you are the son
Of the living God dwelling in me
Making me see your hearts in mine
I am yours

Good shepherd come and your sheep to lead
You know us well and all our needs
It was for us that you suffered much
We bow to you we worship you
We adore you lord our God.

Chapter 8

Scripture

God was manifest in the flesh

Justified in the spirit

Seen by angels

Preached among the gentiles

Believed on in the world

Received up in glory

Now the spirit expressly says in latter times

Some will depart from faith

Giving heed to deceiving spirits and doctrines of

Demons speaking lies in hypocrisy having their

Own conscience seared with a hot iron, forbidding people to marry and commanding them to abstain from foods which God created to be received with thanksgiving

by those who believe and know the truth.

for every creature of God is good and nothing is to be refused if it is received with thanksgiving.

That the genuiness of your faith being much more
Precious than gold that perishes though it is tested by fire
may be found to praise, honour and glory at the revelation of Jesus Christ.

Whom having not seen your love, though now you do not see him yet believing
    you rejoice with joy inexpressible
And full of glory.
Exercising loving kindness, judgment and righteousness
In the earth, for in these the lord delights

The goodness of God brings us first to repentance so
We can be sanctified and purified.

Testimony

My niece was put into care at a very young age, I still had two boys at home so when my niece asked me if she could stay with me I said I haven't got the room. a few years after this

My eldest son moved out as he got married. my niece came to visit and said that she was pregnant and didn't have anywhere to stay. The only room we had was a put you up bed in my youngest sons bedroom, during this time my youngest son and my niece became more like brother and sister, they would argue about who was going to sleep in the bed and who would be on the put you up bed my husband and myself would pray with my niece and tell how much her heavenly father loves her, there is always hope in Jesus Christ and thankfully my niece got a home of her own and had a beautiful baby boy.

We led my niece through the prayer of salvation, excellent, it was a great pleasure to be able to minister to my niece in this time.

One day my niece came to visit she hadn't been with me long when her mobile phone started to ring,

My niece answered and I could hear her talking but I didn't know to who, suddenly she burst out crying and said I'll pass the phone to my auntie, I can't speak to you,

I took the phone and there was a lady crying, I asked her what is your name, she told me and I carried on to say I don't know if you have ever heard about Jesus Christ,

She must of thought I was stark raving mad, but she said yes a bit at school, then she carried on to say that she was in a lot of pain, bleeding and was loosing her baby.

I said I lift you up right now that the pain will leave you,

Your baby will be safe and the bleeding will stop, she said that she felt something then but she didn't know what it was, she said I am out side the doctors now and I have to go in, I said put your trust in Jesus Christ and that was that, my niece and myself carried on talking when about half an hour had past when her mobile went again my niece was talking and saying oh no then my niece passed her phone to me and as she passed the phone she said the doctors have said she has lost her baby, I took the phone and the lady was crying, she said yes the doctor has said I have lost my baby and I am on my way to the hospital for an emergency d.n.c I said, no you are still pregnant.

The pain will go and the bleeding will stop, also I said if you break your arm the doctor will send you for an x ray and go by that, but you are going with the unseen and putting your trust in our lord Jesus she said the pain had eased off a bit and should she still go to the hospital, I said yes, when the doctors confirm that you are still pregnant our father gets the glory. well this time about three hours passed when my nieces phone went again, my niece was crying, she kept saying oh I'm sorry, this time I just took the phone, the lady said the doctor had done some tests and said you have lost your baby and we need you to come in for an emergency d.n.c. I said no you are still pregnant your baby is safe, she said she didn't know what to think, I said I no its hard but keep trusting in the Lord, my niece then shouted at me she said you are not listening she has lost her baby I said no, you are not listening her baby is safe.

It came to the time for my niece to leave and although I had seen my niece over the next few months it had gone completely out of my mind about the young lady, then one day a knock went at the door, a lady was standing there, I must have had a puzzled look on my face as I said come in she said you don't remember me do you,

I said sorry no I don't, she said you prayed for me when I was told I had lost my baby and I wanted to thank you and as you can see I am still pregnant patting her lump.

We spent time together and I led her through the prayer of salvation, excellent.

Poem

This is a poem that my niece has written.
When I look back on the years
It was you mum who fought the tears
When I needed you most of all
It was you mum who caught my fall
When I gave birth to my gorgeous boys
It was you mum who brought them
special toys.

I love you mum more than you know
My love for you will always flow
I need you to know what you mean to me
I want you to feel what I can see
To live your life with no regrets
Because mum it isn't over yet

And when that saddest day does come
And nothing more can be done
I will have to say my goodbyes to
You mum
But only for a short while

For on that day I will cry
Father my lord of heaven and earth
Please take care of my mum
My love for you will remain in my heart
And I know yes I know we are raised up
In Jesus never to be apart.

Chapter 9

Testimony crystal clear

I had just finished writing my song obsolete the tabernacle was prepared, when after weeks of praying and asking for some kind of revelation or something that I could confirm that I was being led by the Holy Spirit and not just me as I kept saying anyone can write songs.

One morning after doing our shopping my husband said do you want to look round the market before we go home,

I said yes we can have a quick look. I wasn't really interested in walking around so we passed a lot of the stalls.

We both stopped in front of one stool that had a lot of different items for sale, my husband picked up something and said do you want this I said no, my husband said it's the Lords supper, I said yes. The assistant took it away put it into a bag.

When we got home I just left the bag on the side in the kitchen, later on in the evening I was going through the song when my husband came in with a box in his hand, I said what is that as he handed me the box, he said this is what we bought from the market, I had just read on the song, pure river of water clear as crystal, I took a box out of the bag that my husband had handed to me, it had written on the box crystal clear with the last supper inside

Excellent.

Song

Obsolete the tabernacle was prepared.
Obsolete the tabernacle was prepared the Holy Spirit
indicating the way into the holiest of all
Was not yet manifest while the first was still standing
To you who's commandments are pure enlightening to the
eyes the fear of the lord is clean enduring forevermore
You who's judgments are true and righteous altogether
Desired more much more than gold sweeter than honey
To you who came to fulfil scripture to bring the truth to
all mankind new covenant in your own blood sealed for many redemption of sin.

The shepherd was struck, the sheep of the flock scattered,
King of the Jews nailed with you, it is finished the spoken word from you then
    you gave up your spirit.
Arise you did resurrection of life the lion of the tribe
Of Judah the root of David you have redeemed us to God
with the shedding of your own blood.

The trumpet blasts the bells are ringing the singers
singing Lord thou art my God

You who makes your spirit angels your ministers a flaming star you who makes
the clouds your chariots
You who walks upon the wings of the wind
All your strings are in thee king king of kings
Pure river of water clear as crystal proceeding from
The throne of God and of the Lamb
Lord God Almighty just and true are your ways
Who shall not fear you and worship your name
For you alone are worthy

The drums are beating the harp and the players playing
The singers singing oh my lord you are my God.

Father you have the authority over all the earth
Hosanna in the highest Lord you are my God.

Poem come and let us reason

Come and let us reason together
The word of God
Jesus Christ is faithful
He said I am faithful and
I am just.

Don't deceive yourselves and
Think that you don't sin
Receive the good news
Let Jesus Christ your Lord
Your saviour in

Be baptized in the name
Of the Father the son and
The Holy Ghost yes
Everyone of you
For it is written
In the word of God

The refiners pot is for silver
The furnace for gold
But the Lord tests our hearts
Have faith and hope as you grow

Although our sins are scarlet
They shall be as white as snow
Though they be red crimson
They shall be as pure gold.

Scripture

Who shall separate you from
the love of Christ
Shall trouble, hardship, persecution, famine,
Danger, or sword.

As it is written
For your sake we face death all day long
We are considered as sheep
To be slaughtered

We are more than conquerors
Through him who loves us
Neither death nor life neither
Angels nor demons neither
The present nor the future

Nor any powers
Neither height nor depth
Nor anything else in all
Creation will be able to
Separate you from the love of God
That is in Jesus Christ our Lord

Chapter 10

Testimony

My husband and my self knew a young lady for years, she spent a lot of time with our granddaughters mum and they became very good friends. She always said she would love to have children but, when the time was right for her, it didn't matter how hard they tried she never got pregnant, the doctors started to do tests and tried different kinds of medication but still nothing, the doctors told her she will never have children but carried on with some more tests, this was going to be the last lot of tests that they could do for her. On hearing this news as you can imagine she was very up set, she was at our granddaughters house when we went to visit, we had always spoke to her about the love of God and how much Jesus Christ loves her, how Jesus was put to death, and wanted a close relationship with her through the Son to our Father. After years of ministering to her she said that she believed and wanted to say the pray of salvation.

Father I come to you as I am

I am sorry and repent for the things in my life that are wrong.

And ask you to forgive me

I believe that you came in the flesh

That you were born of the virgin Mary

You shed your blood for me

You died and rose again on the third day

You sit at the right side of the glory of God

My father

Jesus please welcome me into your kingdom as one of your own. a-men

There is a rejoicing in heaven as someone confesses

our Lord Jesus Christ. hallelujah.

Well the lady asked my husband and myself to pray for her, we did, and I said I will get you a prayer cloth from our church, she asked what is that, we explained that everyone in the church will stand together in agreement for the same prayer and it shall be done, when we saw her again we gave her the prayer cloth, she said I am going to put it under my pillow, I will keep it there always.

We saw her again a few weeks later and said she had the results to the last of tests and said she has to come to terms with the fact that she will never have children of her own, we said, that's quite often the way, when there seems to be no hope there is always hope in our Lord keep trusting Jesus Christ. When we saw her again a few months had past and thankfully she was pregnant.

She went on to have a healthy baby boy, the doctors couldn't understand how this could have happened but said it will not happen again. as her baby grew she said I would like another baby could you pray for me, we said yes, also I said we will get another prayer cloth, no its alright she said I have still got the first one under my pillow we said just receive from Our Lord then, the next time we saw her she was pregnant again and went on to have another healthy baby boy.

My granddaughter says every time she sees the eldest boy he is reading the bible and always wants to talk about God.

What a blessing.

Two poems that I have written
I have commanded

I have commanded it stood fast
I fashion individually my laws I write on their hearts
From the place of my dwelling I spoke it was done
Father in heaven your kingdom come

Give a drink to him who thirst
If hungry feed him know that it is i
I am he on hearing my word believe believe in me

Put my yoke upon you learn from me
I am gentle in spirit your sins I cast into the sea
I remember no more sin or iniquities
Know that I am I am he

The light is already shinning
Darkness is passing away
Love your brother abide in the light
Don't go astray

Through the vail that is Jesus Christ flesh
Beautiful in elevation enter into the holiest
Let you fountain be blessed
Rise up to the heavens and you will see
My glory for I delight in mercy
New wine filled with righteousness
When the son of man sits on the throne
Of glory in the regeneration with
Loving kindness.

Time is passing by

Time is passing by just like the wind and the rain
Your holy spirit does the same I am amazed
Your spirit goes wherever he goes with joy peace all
Power from you and as I come before you I say
Oh what a shame
There are thousands that still do not know you
And believe in who you say you are
But if we don't have faith and hope in you
Well we might just as well be dead.

You're the lamb the chosen one of God al-le-lu-ia-a-men
When the rain stops and the sun brakes through I
Remember the words that you spoke and that you
Are the bright and morning star and I praise and love you.

Your eyes as flames of fire the many crowns upon your
Head for on your white horse you will be
Charging to victory with your new name the word of God
And from your mouth a sharp sword
And as I come before you I say I am amazed.

We grow up like children before you we learn all
Your ways for you were both human and divine
All glory to you Jesus and at the end of all things
The lion will lay down with the lamb you will rule
And care for your sheep forever with eternal peace
All my adoration goes to you.

I just stand as I look to you and I am amazed at the
Amazing things that you do for God has blessed us
by opening our ears and minds to receive you
And I am amazed we only live because of you
From the start until the end I will have faith and hope
In you father son holy spirit we thank you almighty God
Eternal father what a privilege it is knowing you and
As I come before you I say I am amazed.

Chapter 11

Three songs that I have written England sings

Here in this land this land that we love
England sings
Give thanks to God our father
For Elizabeth she is our queen
Scotland Wales Ireland join into
As we sing this song to you
A special gift from heaven above
Sealed for Elizabeth

Queen of our country with love
In our hearts
The national flag of red white and blue
Be filled with the spirit of our living God
A fresh anointing on you

A chosen generation a royal priesthood
The word of God
With blessings to our Queen
Queen Elizabeth
We salute you in love yes we salute you in love.

Faith shall breathe

Take my life lord let it be ever consecrated to thee
Take my voice Lord that I may sing forever only to my king, you are the root
    and offspring
And faith shall breathe her glad a-men a-men lord a-men
Anointing from the holy one alleluia a-men

Keep your will oh keep it thine father no longer mine
Your will be done, Abba father keep me faithful to your son
And faith shall breathe her glad a-men a-men Lord a-men
You are the first you are the last alleluia a-men

Son of man keep my heart its your own never apart eternal father your royal
throne bride of the bridegroom cry come
And faith shall breathe her glad a-men a-men lord a-men
You are the beginning you are the end alleluia a-men

As every command lord you make of me gloriously unfolds you are reflected
in me, my spirit responds in harmony when my great God says, be still
surely I am coming quickly
And faith shall breathe her glad a-men a-men lord a-men
Clear as crystal is your love for me in spirit and in unity the spirit and the
bride cry come my lord, even so, come Lord Jesus come lead us to the holy
city the new Jerusalem
Keep my heart lord, keep it thine own, it is now your royal throne.

My God in Christ

You are my God my God in Christ
Reconciling the world to yourself
You who knew no sin
Became sin for us all
That we might become the righteous
Of God in him.

I bring myself as an offering
With a pure heart I will praise my king
The foundations of pure gold
Let you clear clear waters flow

I worship you my God
For the testimony of Jesus
Is the spirit of prophecy in truth
Through the veil into the holiest
I declare you lord of all

I bring myself as an offering
With a pure heart I will praise my king
The foundations of pure gold
Let your clear clear waters flow.

Scripture

Before faith came we were kept under guard by the law
Kept for faith which would afterwards be revealed
Therefore the law was our tutor to bring us to Christ
That we might be justified by faith

But after faith has come we are no longer under
A tutor, for you are all sons of God through faith in Jesus Christ, Jews or Greek
    male or female All are heirs according to the promise but when the fullness
    of time has come God sent forth his son born of a woman born under the
    law to redeem those who were under the law that we might receive the
    adoption as sons
God has sent forth his spirit the spirit of his son into our hearts crying Abba
    father.

Chapter 12

❧

Testimony

Song I have written come out of the world.

My nephew always wanted to come to live with us, as just like my niece he was put into care.

He knocked on the door one evening, it looked as if he hadn't had a wash for weeks, my husband and myself tried to find out, what had been going on with him in the past few weeks but we couldn't make out what he was talking about, we decided to let him stay for the night and have a chat with him in the morning.

Both my husband and myself had to go to work, my nephew was still a sleep so we thought we would leave him there and see him later.

When I got in from work my nephew hadn't moved out of the bed all day, I said you need to drink and eat but he didn't want to come down stars, he was talking a bit better than the night before but it took weeks before my nephew explained that he has been told that he has mental health problems and the medication that he has been taking makes him feel like a zombie.

As the days went on we found out that he did have a team of people helping him, and my nephew started to talk about the places that he had lived, the things that he felt were wrong, my husband and myself would talk to him about the love of God and how much Jesus Christ loves him, at this time he would always say there isn't any God, if there was why do people kill each other and why are there wars and why do children die.

The best way, to try and explain to my nephew was put it this way, you get to an age where you go into rebellion we think we know better than our parents, we want to do things our way, even when our parents want us to go another way because they know it's the best for us.

Our father in heaven is the same he has given us free will,

He says choose me and live.

But we think we know better than our creator, we want to go our own way, Jesus said he is the way the truth and the life.

Over the next few weeks we ministered to my nephew, he started spending more time down stars and although he still had a lot of issues to sort out he started to look happy.

Family and people at our church was lifting my nephew up in prayer and one day as I came in from work he was reading my bible, he started being interested and wanted to know the answers to a lot of questions, my husband and myself thought, brilliant, it wasn't easy but this went on for two years until someone who we knew offered my nephew a room in a house just around the corner from ourselves, I didn't think my nephew was ready but he was so excited and always wanted a place of his own. He thought this would be good for his own independence.

My husband and myself explained to my nephews landlord that to motivate my nephew you have to talk him through the tasks that he has to do, he said he would be going around to check on him to make sure he is alright but it wasn't long before, one day when I came in from work there was a letter waiting for me saying my nephew hadn't done the washing up, and he hadn't done something else.

My husband and my-self went round to see my nephew, we had a chat with him and tidied up.

Before my nephew moved into this home he said the prayer of salvation, he received the love of the truth.

And said he believed Jesus Christ was his Lord and saviour.

My husband and myself was trying to find ways that my nephew could get into some sort of routine to complete the tasks that he had to do on a daily basis, but without anyone being with him things were being left and this resulted into his landlord writing another letter saying this is the last time he is going to write my nephew will have to leave, the funny thing about that was my nephew really liked him and could understand what he was saying but was unable to carry things through.

A few days past when my nephews landlord came around to visit my husband and myself he said he wanted my nephew to move out at the weekend, he also went on to say I thought you said he has said the prayer of salvation, I said yes he has, my nephews landlord carried on to say well he didn't mean it,

I said you know the word of God judge and examine yourself, the measure of judgement you give others is the measure our heavenly father gives to us.

Also I said Jesus didn't come for the righteous, but the unrighteous, he didn't come for the saved he came for the lost, and as its written nobody can confess that I came in the flesh unless they are from God.

And if we think that we don't sin we only deceive ourselves.

While my nephew was living there he met a girl, they were very happy together, after spending some time with my nephews girlfriend she to received the love of the truth, excellent, they went on to have a beautiful baby boy and then after one problem after another my nephew was put into prison.

My husband and myself would go to visit and take my nephews girlfriend sometimes, when he came out of prison he was put into a hospital for mental health patients.

In all this time my nephew wanted his mail to come to our address as he never knew where he would be next, we carry on praying for him.

The good news, he has a place of his own, and he will be raised up in Christ Jesus our Lord we give our thanks.

After starting to write this my nephew had a bit of trouble, he was told he had lost his flat, also he was told that he would not be offered another place to live, he spent a few days with my husband and myself, we could spend time ministering to him, we are Gods own creation and he knows his own, we have every faith that our father will lead my nephew through the power of the holy spirit to present him blameless in Jesus Christ. We carry on praying for my nephew and we have told him we love him. Also I have said that when he sleeps on the couch this is not good for him or anyone really its alright when its just for two or three nights but no more. I keep looking at the verse in the bible where it it written I have plans for you not to harm you but you would prosper and our hope would be that for everyone they would prosper in the truth as people perish from the lack of knowledge.

Song come out of the world

Come out of the world today
And learn about the way
Put down that pint of beer
Let your saviour draw near
Learn to live without your drugs
Seek help from the Lord your God
Get high in the spirit and seek
For the things from above

Come out of the world today
Put your hands together and pray
Give me strength oh Lord each day
So that I can obey

The kingdom of heaven
Is at hand let God hold you in his
Mighty hand grow in the love of God
Your father in heaven above

So come out of the world today
Give your thanks and your praise
Open up your eyes and you will see
Everlasting life for eternity.

Chapter 13

Testimony—Greatest testimony of all

Come and listen to the testimony of our God
Come and listen to the testimony of our God
It's the greatest testimony of them all
It comes from above
Three in heaven bear witness to the truth
The Father the Son the Holy Ghost
These three are one
And they testify of the risen son
Son of man on the third day raised to life
Jesus the resurrection of life.

The bread we partake of is the living bread
It's the body and the flesh of our
Lord Jesus Christ.
The bread that's faithful and true
You dwell in him and he dwells in you
And through Gods Son everlasting life he gives to you
He gives this gift to you.

Three bear witness to the truth on the earth.
The Spirit the Water the Blood
These three will agree in one
And they testify of the blood shed
From Gods only son

The water is a well of water springing up into everlasting life
For it is written and its true
Let the light live in you
Forever be with you God.

An everlasting covenant

Satan take your hands off the children of God
They are washed by Jesus Christ own blood
They are redeemed yes redeemed by the lamb of God

They will sing praises to their king
The son of man they will lift him high
They are filled with my fathers Great grace Great power
And my fathers Great love
They have an everlasting covenant an everlasting love.

Satan flee from the children—children of
Their Great God
They have been bought with a price
With the precious blood of Jesus Christ.

They will move with my fathers Great grace Great power
And my fathers Great love
They have an everlasting covenant an everlasting love

Satan your time is at an end leave
For the righteous of God are full of the anointing
They will preach the word of God
They will mend the broken hearted they will
Set the captives free

They will sing praises to their king
The son of man they lift him high
They are filled with my fathers Great grace Great power
And my fathers Great love
They have an everlasting covenant an everlasting love

Chapter 14

Scripture In whom are hid all Treasures

In whom are hid all Treasures.

In whom are hid all Treasures of wisdom and knowledge

And this I say, lest any man should beguile you with

Enticing words.

For though I be absent in the flesh, yet I am with you in the spirit, joying and
beholding your order and the sted fastness of your faith in Christ Jesus the
Lord, so walk in him, rooted and built up in him and established in faith
as you have been taught.

Abounding therein with thanksgiving.

Beware, lest any man spoil you through philosophy and vain deceit after the
rudiments of the world and not after Christ, for in him Dwell'eth all the
fullness of the Godhead bodily and ye are complete in him, which is the
head of all

Principality and power.

Put on therefore as the elect of God holy beloved bowels of meekness,
longsuffering and even as Christ forgave you, so also do ye, above all things
put on charity which is the bond of perfectness and let the peace of God
rule in your heart.

And in all things be thankful

How many times

How many times do I come before your throne
And ask you to forgive me
Father I am sorry for the things that I do wrong
Have mercy on me oh Lord have mercy on me.

Every thought I think of that's not of you i
Know its an obomination to you
I stand before you trembling inside
Weak no strength to be found my face towards
The ground, then I am on my knees
Father my Lord my God have mercy on me.

Your right hand leads and holds me
You raise my head and you say
How many times do I ask you to forgive
That's how many times ill forgive you
The truth has set you free

The path of the righteous shall not be moved
The root of the righteous is a tree of life
And he that winneth souls is wise
With joy you will draw water from the wells of salvation
My people will turn to me.

Faith should not stand in the wisdom of men
But in the power of God
Examine and judge yourselves let the Lord build your house.
For the potter has power over all the clay for
the same lump to make one vessel.

Sing to the Lord for he has done excellent things
Praise and declare his deeds
For our father gives the increase
Rejoice for Jesus of Nazareth is the Prince of Peace

For the greatest love story

For the Greatest love story ever told
Was about God our Fathers love for us
The word—Jesus Christ became flesh
Over 2000 years ago—hallelujah a—men

We praise you Lord for your mighty acts
For you inhabit the praises of the saints
We sing aloud dance and exalt your mighty
Name—clap our hands and make a joy full
Sound to all the ends of the Earth we will
Sing and dance just for you—Jesus of Nazareth
We love you.

All nations will turn and bow before you
For they will come to reco'gnise no other
Name will do because salvation belongs to you.
Jesus all power is given to you in heaven and of the earth, John the baptise
     baptized with water but you Jesus baptized with the Holy Ghost and fire.

All glory and honour for of him and through him and to him are all things.
All glory and honour to the Lamb hallelujah a—men

Chapter 15

Scripture I have come as a light

I have come as a light

Therefore they could not believe, Isaiah said he has blinded their eyes and hardened their hearts lest they should see with their eyes lest they should understand with their hearts and turn so that I should heal them.

Then Jesus cried out and said

He who believes in me, believes not in me but in him who sent me

And he who sees me, sees him who sent me.

I have come as a light into the world, that whoever believes in me should not abide in darkness and if anyone hears my words and does not believe, I do not judge him,

For I did not come to judge the world, but to save the world.

My sister Debbie

My sister has lung cancer and was told she had about five years to live. The doctors started Debbie on her treatment.

And although feeling very tired and weak wanted to still go to work, with the first treatment the doctors were hoping to reduce the size of the tumour in her lung and get rid of some of the modules but after the first treatment was over Debbie and her husband Geoff were told that there hadn't been any change, obviously all the family have been praying for healing and we all prayed over a prayer cloth at the church my husband and myself attend, my sister was looking more and more weaker and finding it hard to breath, the doctors wanted to try something else, but after doing more tests they found the tumour had grown in size and my sister has small ones in her chest. At this point my sister was told that she has got three to six months to live. She was finding it harder and harder to walk, even getting out of her car and walking to the lift at work so she eventually gave up work.

I have said to Debbie if you have faith as small as a mustard seed it can move mountains, so we say to this cancer be removed in Jesus Christ name. Debbie always says she is sorry if she is upset I told her if you cry I will cry with you and if you laugh I will laugh with you it doesn't matter does it.

Geoff has asked his work if he could have time off to spend with Debbie and my brother and sister in law have been fantastic at sorting out paper work and just being there to support them both. They just live across the road from Debbie and Geoff so they pope in more or less each day to make sure they are alright.

I keep speaking the word of God to Debbie because against all hope there is hope in Jesus Christ

When the doctors say there is nothing more they can do for you but make you more comfortable

When you feel like your so weak you cannot go on for another day.

The Holy Spirit will be your strength the Lord will here your cry. My sister has told me that when its your time to go you will and she has excepted the fact that she is dying

At the moment she is putting her house in order, she says it will make it easier for Geoff when she is not there she must find it very hard when I am saying I am waiting for the Lord to heal your disease and the doctors tell her something different and she can hardly breathe. This has given my son the motivation to do a run for cancer research and my youngest sister and her children a run for life.

The good news is that Debbie has decided to be confirmed

Within the next two weeks and although everyone else are being confirmed three months latter the vicar said he would confirm Debbie by herself with all her family there. we can all welcome Debbie into our fathers kingdom. people at the church will do something to eat and drink for everyone, fantastic.

The next song I have written is especially for Debbie that our worship leader is going to put music to the words and then the plan is to get all the people that attend our church to sing it while I film it. Terry and myself picked up my mum and step dad, went to visit Debbie and Geoff I said I would do a chilli and rice for lunch although I didn't think Debbie would eat any as she was finding it hard to swallow so she was on soups, also Geoff would carry Debbie down stares, when she felt she had enough breathe to be lifted and the slight touch of anyone would be very pain full for Debbie but she could look out of her big windows in her front room and look at her garden but she kept saying all she can see is green, there is no colour I said we will get you some plants and put them in your pots. We went to the garden centre and picked up everything we could see with colour my mum spent time with Debbie and making the drinks for us all while terry me and Reg, my step dad, went into the garden, terry decided to do the weeds around the boarder as Reg and me well more Reg was potting the plants. Geoff showed us where he wanted the pots to go, the best place for Debbie to see them.

It started to rain so I said, lets go in now but terry and Reg carried on determined to finish what we had started.

My mum was looking after the chilli and when it was time to dish up Geoff said Debbie does want some chilli, I was so pleased as she eat it all with a bit of garlic bread and she managed a desert it couldn't have been a better day.

Geoffs brother in law has been doing their on sweet bathroom so Debbie can have a seat in the shower that she cannot wait for also they are having a stare lift put in to make it easier for Debbie and Geoff to get down stairs and up again. I was listening to her talk the other day, my brother has sorted out all her finances and she was saying I don't want to go on with no quality of life and if I am healed that's different from being like this, she has chosen the songs she wants sung at her funeral, she has worked out exactly how its all going to be done, she said I want to spend the night here, that was at St Georges church where Debbie and Geoff have been attending with my brother and sister in law. Then she said I am going to be cremated in Bracknell and then I want to go to Ashford cemetery long lane as our brother and other members of our family are there to. Every day is a battle for her but I thought what an inspiration she is.

There is a new bishop for the reading area who when Debbie was confirmed wanted to be there, quite a lot of other people wanted to come as well. Debbie looked lovely you could here that she still had her sense of humour as she was sitting in her wheel chair with a new pair of shoes on everyone was saying how nice the shoes were when she put out her leg and said I will never be able to walk in them. She always has made me laugh it's the way she says things and if she is with my brother well its just one laugh after another. The whole service was very good my brother read a piece of scripture and we had a laugh when the bishop sprinkled water over Debbie, she wanted more.

On Sunday our worship leader sang the song I have written for Debbie, I cried all the way through it so I had to leave the filming of it to terry and they sang another song that I wrote we sing hallelujah to you lord, now its trying to get it all together and put on a D.V.D, so I can give it to Debbie and Geoff.

our worship leader has to shorten the words to fit in with the tune but it is excellent and I cannot thank them all enough. my youngest son is doing the half marathon on Sunday for Debbie and his dad

I want to film this also and try to do the D.V.D with the two songs, the run for cancer and some pictures taken from Debbie's confirmation, I don't know how this will turn out. I am really hoping that this week will be good for Debbie, her nurse will be going in and they are going to sort out an oxygen tank also she is hoping that they will drain her lungs and put in a catheter

So she won't have to keep injecting her morphine into her stomach which gets bruised. she is taking steroids but this is like everything else when would be the best time to take these as she gets very tired. i keep crying out to my lord to heal Debbie's disease as the word tells me, what ever you ask and do not doubt it shall de done, in my name, so I cry out yeshua, abba father we rebuke this cancer and ask for the release of your holy spirit in the mighty name of Jesus Christ thank you lord. I am so glad that the bishop said about the things that we must do, repent and Debbie did that and he went on, I thought that's the same as the prayer of salvation and I know our father will welcome Debbie into his kingdom through the believe in Jesus Christ of Nazareth his son forever.

Next is the song Divine child of mine as it is written for the music

What can I do what can I say
You feel your life might be slipping away
I will hold you close close in my arms
You are my child divine
I will keep you safe not just for today
But for eternity you are a child a child of mine
You are my child divine

Forever and always I will love you
Child of mine
You are so special to me
I will walk with you across the golden sand
And we'll bathe in the clear blue sea
You are my child divine.

When you cry I will cry with you
I will send my comforter
I see the suffering you are going through
Because you are the child of mine
I will strengthen you not just for today
But for eternity you are a child a child of mine
You are my child divine

Rest in me when you feel weak
I will raise you up today
It was on that cross that I died to set you free
You are a child of mine
I will carry you not just for today
But for eternity you are a child a child of mine
You are my child divine
You are a child of mine you are my child divine.

Divine child of mine

What can I do for you what can I say to you
For your life might be slipping away from you
I will hold you close, close in my arms
You are a child of mine child of mine you are divine
I will keep you safe not just for today but for eternity too
Child of mine I am always with you.

Forever and always I love you child of mine you are special to me I will raise
you up and then one day you may say you are my God Jesus healed my
disease you are my Lord you died for me.

When you cry I will cry with you
I will send my comforter to comfort you
I see the suffering you are going through
I know its difficult for you
Child of mine I will carry you

Forever and always I love you child of mine you are special to me. I will raise
you up and then one day you may say you are my God Jesus healed my
disease you are my Lord you died for me.

Rest in me when you feel weak
And you think life is so bleak
I will strengthen you I will hold your hand
Together we will walk across the golden sand
We will take a dip in the blue blue ocean
And bathe in the clear blue sea
Child of mine I will cleanse you thoroughly

Forever and always I love you child of mine you are special to me I will raise
you up and then one day you may say you are my God Jesus healed my
disease you are my Lord you died for me.
I am true ill take good care of you

Divine child of mine I will always love you

My mum told Debbie that she had sent away to the woodland Trust to have a tree planted for Debbie and on the certificate it says our daughter Deborah Ann Habgood

For the courage, strength and fortitude shown by our Debbie aged fifty three fighting terminal lung cancer over this last year God bless

My mum and step dad had been staying with Debbie and Geoff but because they both had to be somewhere on Tuesday morning they decided to go home Monday night, my brother was going to pick them up when he finished work to take them back,

I thought terry and myself will pop over just after lunch to see Debbie and Geoff I thought it would break the day up for them but as I got there and looked at Debbie who was not speaking her eyes were half way showing, her feet were so cold and hard, every now and then Debbie would shout out ah-ah-ah-.i said I know Deb, we know, be at peace. The nurse had told my mum no one knows how long Debbie's got she could go two or three weeks. When I got home I phoned my mum to see what time my brother was going to take them back and to try and warn my mum how Debbie was.

When I came off the phone I was so angry and upset, my eldest son went outside and sat on the step, I followed him out and I looked up at the sky and said to my son, you know I have been praying for healing for Debbie but she is suffering so much and yet we have a merciful and compassionate God but i said I don't see any compassion or mercy my son looked up at me and said your prayers have been heard Debbie will go today. My son said look at the sky how nice it is Debbie want suffer any more. Well we went to get some petrol and my mum phoned to say Debbie had past away at five fifty my my managed to be there to hold her hand

5.50—8th May 2012—
Debbie's funeral 31st may 2012
We all love and miss Debbie very much.
She was very brave she was stunning xxx

Chapter 16

This is my husbands story

My earliest memory of going to church was with my eldest sister taking me to the mission hut at the end of our road,

Where I joined the woodcraft and then I joined the boys brigade which was held in the same hut.

On and off I would go to St Marys church that was in the village, this didn't last long as I went of to the scouts, which was held in the Vicarage grounds at st marys in the meantime, my mum and dad fostered two of my cousins a boy and a girl. To give my mum and dad a rest we all had to go to church on a Sunday afternoon leaving my mum and dad to have a sleep.

After church we all had to go to our grandparents. in our Sunday best. We weren't aloud to play out like the other kids in our street.

At the age of thirteen I joined the sea cadets until I was sixteen and a half so church was out at this time apart from the odd remembrance Sunday and the odd church parade. I started working at the Middlesex and surrey laundries as a van boy when I left school, I was working with a driver called Bill, and over time Bill and his wife became very special to me, I trusted them, as my confidence went when I was molested when I was about eleven years of age, I couldn't tell my parents as I was frightened that they would tell me off as I shouldn't have been so far away from home. and I was worried about getting a good hiding

When we called at his house we had tea and sandwiches, when he had to go into hospital for an operation I had to go to work with other drivers, some of them were quite terrible, eventually I left but I still went round Bill's house to see him and his wife vi who was lovely lady.

The last time I saw him he was about ninty years old.

At the age of eighteen I was searching, I thought shall I go to the church of England, Catholic then i stumbled across evangelical which seemed to be what i was looking for, i met a young lady who i felt a lot for but it went wrong and at the age of twenty one i went into a depression.

I vowed i would never fall for anyone again. i worked in various places and at the age of nineteen I had a job on the airfreight, having lived right outside Heathrow airport it took me all over the country. i met lots of famous people and had some strange consignments to deliver. one of the consignments were a couple of cartons of books to be placed in Bromley kent, to the children of God, they helped me unload the van and when we had finished asked me to lift my hands in the air and say out loud I love Jesus so I did, then went on my way, not thinking much more about it. and at the age of twenty three I got a driving job for a big printing company, I was off work for a while with a slipped disc, towards the end of my time off I started to go for long walks about ten miles, it was on one of these walks that I came across a magazine called back to the Godhead which is a publication of the hare Krishna movement I sat and read it, this started my brain ticking over again and I went to the mind body and spirit exhibition at olimpia, London, and found out about different religions but still i could not commit myself. my mother knew a lot of people in our village and sold a wardrobe to someone we'de known for years, after a while I started going round to his house regular with another friend of mine. all three of us were well into taking drugs and drink. I would sometimes take the children to the park or swimming just to get a break. This was when he introduced me to his ex wife, Teresa, Both of us didn't want any commitment but it was if the further apart we wanted to be the closer we were getting.

Eventually after six years like that, we married. But before we married I prayed one night for forgiveness as i was on drink and drugs and asked for the Lords help to take away the drink and the drugs for me, and I thank the Lord that although it was difficult I made it.

we both believe in God the father the son and the holy spirit but never went anywhere although we had been praying about this, we would have Jehovah witnesses round on a regular basis and read the word of God together we enjoyed this very much, also we would read the word of God with the mormons. Then one day Teresa's dad told us about a church in fleet Hampshire that he'd been to, that we started going to.

After the new pastor took over we were invited on to the ministry prayer team, we were invited to a church at four marks in Hampshire, at the end of the service we were asked to go down the front with other members of the ministry team, people in the congregation were asked if they wanted healing, if they did they should make their way to the front.

Teresa started to ask what they needed prayer for and one lady said it was for the spots on her face to go, we laid hands on her and as we moved to someone else the spots started to go /hallelujah. The last person we prayed for was a boy with down syndrome he had been brought to church by his brother and sister they said he has never spoken and they didn't know if he couldn't speak or wouldn't speak, we laid our hands on him and as we finished praying, we started making our way back to our seats when he stopped us and said hello, praise the Lord his sister and brother were so excited, so were we.

The next song I have written

I've been searching for treasure
Its out there I've been told then I found
A treasure that's worth more to me
Than pure gold.

A treasure never ending beyond the eye can see
A treasure from my father
Who gives to me freely.

I welcomed Jesus into my heart
Never to be the same
I received the Holy Spirit
Then I started to proclaim
The ransomed blood of him on high
For sinners to be slained
When I called out to Jesus Christ
Straight away to me he came.

When I am in despair
And nothing is going right
There is trouble all around
I am too weak to fight
He pours out his spirit
To give me strength for each day
This wonderful Lord of mine.
Jesus Christ is his name.
I call out to Jesus Christ
The name above all names
He pours out his spirit
And he comforts me again.

Chapter 17

Testimony thanks giving

I want to give my thanks for such a loving and caring husband, family children
   and grandchildren.

And although both my sons have had difficult times

Received Jesus Christ into their lives as their Lord and saviour.

The same for our grandchildren they all responded at the same time—brilliant.

I hope they will see the Lords face before them always

And the Lord will bless them so they can be a blessing to others.

That they will grow in knowledge and understanding

That they in time will bring the light to many.

That they will know that we love them all very much.

My eldest son and his wife had a baby boy who died, this put a strain on their
   marriage.

They already had an older boy who is fantastic, but found it hard to cope with the death of his brother, they were having a outreach meeting one evening. my son his wife and my grandson came, at the end they asked if anyone would like prayer, they all went down, this was a week for our American brothers and sisters to come over and join in and brothers from Nigeria, it was the lion and the eagle conference, anyway as they started to pray for my son you could see him going down to the floor in slow motion because they was filming this my youngest son said if I didn't know him I would of thought it was put on but because I do know him, I know there is no way he would have gone down like that by himself. he received Jesus Christ. eventually the marriage was over and they got divorced, . . . my grandson lives with my son, and for quite a long time they were depressed. Callum, my grandson kept saying to my son, you need Jesus in your life dad, my son said, it can be quite embarrassing as he used to carry Callum on his shoulders if his legs were aching and shout out you need Jesus dad, on many occasions I would have the God channel on, premier Christian radio, or playing a C.D my Son would be sitting there with tears in his eyes.

As soon as I would walk in the room he would the other way.

There has been many times when my grandson has asked us to pray for him and he just receives from our lord.

I know the Holy Spirit does a work in all of us and hopefully will continue a-men

Scripture I heard a voice from heaven

I heard a voice from heaven
Like the voice of many waters and
Like the voice of a loud thunder and I
Heard the sound of a harpest playing
Their harps

They sang as it were a new song
Before the throne before the four living
Creatures and the elders and no one
Could learn that song except
The hundred and forty four thousand
Who were redeemed from the Earth

It is done I am the alpha and the omega
The beginning and the end
I will give of the fountain of life freely
To him who thirst

Chapter 18

Song He is my king

Every day I know you a bit more I can see what
I could not see before
Your righteousness convicts me of all my sins
But my lord I would not let you in

Everyone was talking about you saying
You're the messiah chosen one their king
I heard what they was saying about you lord
But I was a mocker a hypocrite dead in sin

I cried out abba abba father I love you i
Started to sing my soul magnifies my lord
And I rejoice in God my saviour he is my king

Jesus I came to you as I am I said I am sorry
I repent of my sins I opened my door I welcomed
You in you was with me at the beginning
You will be with me at the end

I cried out abba abba father I love you i
Started to sing my soul magnifies my lord
And I rejoice in God my saviour he is my king

Now I can proclaim that I can claim the
Benefits from my lord I can bless as I have
Been blessed I will sing from my heart and
That's the truth and from my mouth I will
Confess from everlasting to everlasting my
Soul magnifies my lord and I will rejoice
In God my saviour he is my king,

Song
We will sing a new song

We will sing a new song to you lord
Herin herin is love not that we loved God
But that God loves us
For spring is here your leading us to waters a new
God with us we praise you
We sing to the God of Abraham, Jacob and issac
You gave thousands of souls to our ancestors
And although generations and times change
Your word stays the same for all mankind.

You are the God of all flesh before, now and forever
more yes you are the God of flesh forevermore.

Its not about boasting in ourselves
Its not about our Glory
For fleshly things will all pass away
But our fathers love remains the same
Its your will be done not our own
Yes its your will be done.

You hold the seven stars in your right hand
They are the angels of the churches
The candlesticks are the churches
And one fits into the other perfectly

All glory and honour for of him
And to him and through him are all things
All glory and honour to the lamb
Hallelujah a-men.

For he was—he is—and is to come—

Scripture—The veil is taken away

Clearly you are an epistle of Christ,
Ministered by us, written not with ink,
But by the spirit of the living God,
Not on tablets of stone but on tablets of flesh,
That is the heart.

Ministers of the new covenant,
Not of the letter but of the spirit,
For the letter kills,
But the spirit gives life.

The children of Israel could not look
Steadily in the face of moses because
Of the glory of his countenance which
Glory was passing away.
How will the ministry of the spirit,
Not be more glorious.

The ministry of righteousness exceeds,
Much more in glory
But their minds were blinded until this day,
The same veil remains un lifted
In the reading of the old testament
Because the veil is taken away in Christ.
When one turns to the lord, the veil is taken away.
The lord is spirit.

Scripture--first seek after the kingdom of heaven

Because they glorified him not as God neither were they thankful but became
    vain in their imaginations and their foolish heart was darkened professing
    themselves to be wise they became fools
But we know nothing by ourselves but he that judgeth us is the lord
Therefore judge nothing before the time until the lord come, who will bring to
    light the hidden things of the darkness and will make manifest the counsels
    of the hearts and then shall every man have praise of God.
And my speech and my preaching was not of enticing words of mans wisdom
    but in demonstration of the spirit and of power that your faith should not
    stand in the wisdom of men but in the power of God

The eyes of the lord are every where keeping watch on the wicked and the
    good, the tongue that brings healing is a tree of life.
The heavens declare his righteousness and all people
Will see his glory.

Enter into his gates with thanksgiving
And into his courts with praise
Be thankful unto him and bless his name
For the lord is good, his mercy everlasting
And his truth endure'th to all generations.

Finish

Apart from Divine child of mine
He is my king
I've been searching for treasure
All others marvellous light international ministries
Hold the copy rights to,